ABC's for All Ages

A Glance at Dance

Patty Copper

Archway Publishing books may be ordered through booksellers or by contacting:

Archway Publishing
1663 Liberty Drive
Bloomington, IN 47403
www.archwaypublishing.com
1 (888) 242-5904

Interior Image Credit: istick, shutterstock, Ashley Quam

ISBN: 978-1-4808-8499-1 (sc)
ISBN: 978-1-4808-8500-4 (hc)
ISBN: 978-1-4808-8498-4 (e)

Print information available on the last page.

Archway Publishing rev. date: 12/05/2019

Also by Patty Copper

ABC's for All Ages:
Musical Instruments
Take Part in Art
Animals

To One and All

Always TAP your feet

Come join with me using your coordination and agility to boogie, bounce and wiggle.

A is for **A**charuli a playful mood you create

B is for **B**allet getting on your toes is great

The Cha-Cha and the Charleston
it's fun to participate

D is for the Disco Dance
it's an attitude you need

E is for the **E**lectric Slide
laughter is guaranteed

F is for the **F**oxtrot stand up straight and don't let go

G is for Gankino Horo hold hands and follow the flow

H is for the **H**ula and the street dance **H**ip **H**op

The **I**rish **H**ey the male leads
your feet will never stop

J is for the **J**itterbug it is a type of swing

K is for **K**rumping doing chest- pops are the thing

L is for Lyrical where emotions are everything

M is for the **M**oonwalk, the **M**aypole and **M**inuet

Novelty dances are quirky you can even dance with a pet

O is for Odissi you move your torso side to side

P is for the Polka add a little
hop and you'll be satisfied

Q is for the Quickstep
the tempo is very fast

Don't forget the **R**ain Dance
and the **R**umba is a blast

The Shag is a social dance
it's fun to twirl in sand

T is for the **T**wist keep the doo-wop close at hand

U is for **U**nison
dancing together
is quite a show

The **V**iennese **W**altz
is beautiful around
and around you go

Western Dance wear cowboy boots so you can do - si - do

X is for **X**ibelani a fluffy skirt you wear

Dancing the **YMCA** your arms are in the air

The **Z**ambra you are barefoot
so you can dance anywhere

Pick some friends, some boogie shoes, and choose a happy song.

Get on the floor and start to move and you will twirl and soar.

Patty Copper was a high school math teacher for twenty-one years. She lives in Irmo South Carolina, and is enjoying retirement with her husband Mike. Patty has a son and two grandchildren. She is the author of the ABC's for All Ages Series.

Printed in the United States
By Bookmasters